THE OTHER SIDE OF PRAYER

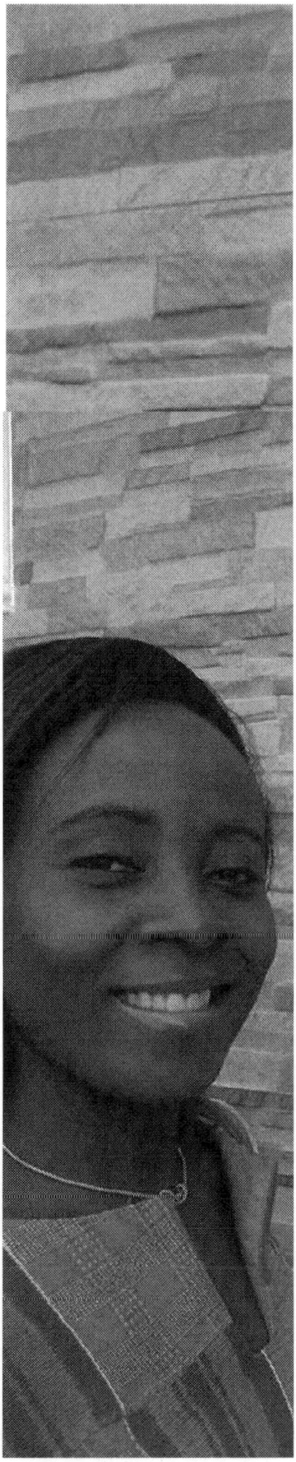

FREDA EYRAM HEWTON

THE OTHER SIDE OF PRAYER

FREDA EYRAM HEWTON

Published by Rhema Publishing
Made in the USA
2016

All scriptures are taken from the Holy Bible King James Version, the New International Version, and other versions.

fredahewton@yahoo.com
fredaadjoahewton@gmail.com
Facebook: Minister Freda Eyram Hewton / Revival Fire
Deliverance Ministries
Shining glory ministry
+233 (0) 247716150/+233 (0) 200204751

ISBN 978-1546565543

Rhema
PUBLISHING

Rhemapublishing1@gmail.com

Dedication

I hereby dedicate this book to the Almighty God, then to My Spiritual Mum, my Mentor Apostle Dr. Denise Thorpe –Revival fire deliverance Ministries Florida USA.

Acknowledgments

In deem of my gratitude and appreciations I, first of all, thank God and all these personalities here for all their support and encouragements throughout my coming up and in ministry with all what God Has deposited inside me for His Kingdom work across the globe. I thank all my father's and my mother here for discovering me and knowing what I carried and helping me to birth all out to the Glory of God. I thank them all for the opportunity, their time, kindness and love. I do sometimes disturb them much as coming up but they have all these years been available for me. I know It wasn't easy but they were always there especially my mentor, I thank her so much for her patience and love all this while. I love all of you and appreciate you all my life no matter where I will be given the opportunity to share whatever I have been made to be in this life according to Gods destiny and purpose for my life, I share all my joy and success with all my father's and mother here. God bless you all much.

Dr.Denise Thorpe My Mentor and Spiritual Mother (Revival Fire Ministries USA), Apostle Nana kwesiDanso(Spiritual Father),Prophet Daniel(head Pastor/father),Pastor Richmond EzeOkezie(Apostle of Prayer),Prophet Nyamekye(prophet Cash) Eagleton Boglo, Pastor Steven (God Father.) Prophetess Linda Akyiaa(Kings and queen) St. Pauls Parish-Christian Daughters Association (Kpehe-Accra), Father Salifu(Saint Pauls Parish), Angel J.Adjapong(Ceo of Yebs Host Ltd),My Mom Mrs.Ernestina Crampah Hewton, My Siblings Freebody Hewton, Ernest and Juliet Crampah. Daniel Osei(shining Glory ministry) ,Mrs. Rosebud Esi Addo, Eunice Boakye, Mr.andMrsBaddoo, Mr.Dampare,

Foreword

Prayer is one of the greatest believers' spiritual weapons of power that guarantees supernatural experience and physical transformation. There is no purpose, vision, or mission executed on earth without prayer and hard work. If prayer wasn't necessary or relevant Jesus Christ wouldn't have prayed nor taught His disciples how to pray. Prayer does what human methods and philosophy cannot do. The absence of prayer is the presence of demonic monopoly, and delays of breakthroughs.

In these last days of human reign and end times, the church must engage more vigorously in holistic intercessory prayers for the salvation of lost souls, and learn to develop an intimate relationship with the Holy Spirit than acquiring earthly possessions and clergy titles. If the church wants to see more of Gods power through the Holy Spirit we have to intensify our prayer lives.

Jesus Christ made a profound statement, 'men ought to pray and faint not'. This statement indicates that prayer should not be sporadic but periodic. If we are going to see God move mightily in our midst we have to pray consistently. Situations may seem to be inexplicable at times to comprehend, but we need to pray like never before. If we want souls to be saved we have to pray. In order to live a successful and meaningful life we have to discover first who we are, know what God is saying to us, be prayerful then work hard to achieve it. There's nothing common in the spirit realms, it takes men who understand the value and possibility of prayer to continually bow their knee in humbleness before God in prayer. The early moves of God's power and Holy Spirit were based on men and woman who devoted their entire lives to prayers, holiness, Gods word and obedience to the voice of the Holy Spirit.

E.M. Bounce said… "What the church needs to-day is not more machinery or better, not new organizations or more and novel methods, but men whom the Holy Ghost can use men mighty in prayer, The Holy Ghost does not flow through methods, but through men. He does come on machinery, but on men. He does not anoint plans, but men-men of prayer."

For the past almost fifteen years of my intercessory prayer life for people and moves of God, I realized that the more closer we are to God the greater we accelerate in the realms of divine hidden packages and experience deeper levels of the supernatural. If we want to experience greater dimensions of the supernatural, we have to totally crucify the flesh, and move in the direction of the Holy Spirit and be obedience to the voice of the Spirit.

This outstanding book will enlighten your understanding on how to engage in proper spiritual warfare against the dark world, rediscover God's purpose, the importance of born gain, most common mistakes we do as Christians, how to reposition one's life in receiving divine results after praying and living a meaningful life, not a meaningless existence.

Freda Eyram Hewton outlined some valuable methods, spiritual insights, and revelations that guarantee immediate results to the prayer of the Christian believer. She's a woman of God filled with the Holy Spirit, and that's one thing I admire about her life.She is an imminent voice of God to humanity in these end time. She said in one of the pages; "Relationship is personal. Your relationship with God has, to begin with, you. A personal one-on-one relationship just like your natural parents. You have to seek and know Him for yourself. A miracle without his word of prayer is baseless."

The pages are filled with revelations, inspirations, revival, and very elevating. You will be blessed by this book and by the end you will have an understanding of the Holy Spirit. The miracles God performed in the days of the Apostles and the reformers are still in operation in today's dispensation. If we can draw closer to God in holiness, prayer, and obedience, we would lack no unction to function under the anointing of the Holy Spirit

Is it revival you need, read this book? Are you thinking God doesn't hear your voice in the spirit realms, or do you struggle to know your originality? then you need to read this book. God hears our prayers when we pray but often the sins we commit blocks the move of God in our lives. The day you quit sinning, and ask forgiveness through God's word, the blood of Jesus Christ will make you whole.

Every pursuit of destiny fulfillment comes with diverse battles and challenges. If you are weak in prayer, the greater your delays become. There are a lot of forces of darkness contending with our destinies. Their mission is to make sure nothing good happens in your life. You cannot overcome them with human-theoretical qualifications, no; you need the power of holistic-prayers to possess what belongs to you through Holy Spirit. No spiritual heights are attained by physical qualifications.

Advice never think daily prayer is a waste of time or energy, no; it's not. That's a deception from the devil. The less you pray the little results you receive. The greater you intensify your prayers, the faster the miracles. According to 1 Kings 18:41-46 "...Elijah said to King Ahab, there's a sound of abundance of rain."

Now, Elijah didn't go-to-sleep or have a cup of coffee for the day, he moved to the God of prayer answering-God. After engaging in seven strategic dimensions of prayers, the heavens opened. What is the lesson here? He gave the prophetic word but activated the word through prayer. Every manifestation of the prophetic word comes through consistent prayer engagement with heaven.

I know you've received several prophecies about your destiny, greatness, and glory, but until you engage yourself in certain realms of effectual fervent prayers, the results can delay. The very day Daniel prayed, his prayers were answered, but it took twenty-one days before the results came (Daniel 9:1-5, 10:11-14). The reason is that the prince of the kingdom of Persia (spiritual realms, not a physical prince) withstood his prayers. This indicates that there are forces of darkness that oppose prayers in the terrestrial and astral realms-the second heavens'. This book is superb! Brilliantly written not by human philosophy, but Holy Spirit filled. Cutting-edge, inspirational and thought-provoking- *"The Other Side of Prayer."*To accomplish your mission, you have to pray. To be who God intended you to be, you have to pray. Nothing is done without prayer. A prayerless Christian is the most spiritual vulnerable believer. Believe it or not, that's the truth.

You cannot be living every-day sinful life, and expect a full-time holy God to work daily miracles in your life. You cannot combat with a full-time devils of darkness whiles still in sin, it's a deception. Your prayers cannot be effective if you are far from God's presence. To genuinely and divinely experience the possibility and *"The Other Side of Prayer'*, then you have to strategically and spiritually reposition your walk with God and relationship with the Holy Spirit. Get a copy, read with spiritual understanding and see God transforming your life for good. Be inspired, be encouraged and be motivated. Divine revelations have no limitations. The possibility and palpability of spiritual breakthroughs in the natural realms is determined by consistent, holistic, and effectual fervent prayers of the righteous.

~Apostle Richmond EzeOkezie /D.D. / B.Th. / Apostle Nana Kwesi Danso Author, Breaking Barriers to Destiny/Maximal Impart Lecturer, Zoe Pastoral & Leadership College Accra-Ghana Founder, Pentecostal Blazing Fire ministries/HagiosAblaze MissionsAfrica, Ghana

Table of Contents

Introduction

There is a blessing in our weakness: there is a blessing in our pain, and sorrowful moments. This time arise so high into aggressive anger, hatred and becomes suicidal. I realized from experience that during these situations, when you feeling helpless, so alone that when God's grace and strength become so strong and sufficient to sustain you. Most people of this current day are in dying need of change, a positive change which only can come from above. The God-given change that overturns every unbearable situation. In the bible, God showed up in a lot of situations of people. This makes most of us wonder in trouble times and it seems like there's no way to the brighter day that we, in turn, asking ourselves so many questions like Lord are you real? Lord why me? When will the Lord ever address my situation?

But let me tell you this God is real. God is the ever sufficient God; Omniscient, Omnipresent, his presence is everywhere, though his manifested presence is not everywhere. Never the less, he is the only true ever faithful God. The only God that made us that we have ever known. In the book of john 1 lets read:

In his word, he is the word; he existed already, he was with the word; and the word was with him. Through him, all things were made. You noticed again; the word was in the world, and though God made the world through him, yet the world did not recognize him. He came to his own, yet again he wasn't recognized. Even in his own country; his own country people did not receive him. Some, however, received him and believed him. As much as Jabez, Hannah knew him in his word and believed in him for an overturn, I have known him in and through his words Jesus Christ our Lord. So God truly visits his people through his son, the highest amongst the kings of this world.

One reason most Christians of today as much as they live are unable to recognize God anytime he visits is, their unaware of recognizing his presence. People as much as Christians need to recognized God's presence more than just a mere feeling. Situations you encounter in a day that you don't get affected in any way; safe sound should alarm you as the doing of the Lord. Never also live your life In the shadow of someone's experience than the word of Lord. Remember the foundations of the world; the earth is as a result of his word.

Some are also saved yet unable to respond to the presence of God. They might be saved, filled with the Holy Spirit, still unable to respond to the presence of the Lord. You may ask why! This is so because they are not in tune and acquainted by the personality of God. His personality is in three. Seriously when you recognize him, and he visits your situation you able to get power through his word to work for you. Mind you the very day you accept Christ, you received power baptism. Unfailing to recognize him, his word, there's no way that power and presence will ever push through to save you. Note, his presence does not have to be the burning bush kind of presence, or earthquake, smoke, thundering. Most people ask these few questions too, must I invite him? Must I go in search of him in the open as a day work out? I believe these are few of most questions that filled hearts of Christians. I advise we look in search; in wait through his word and read examples of the lives of most women and men of God who were able to receive the Lord and with his visitation to them received transformation such as healing, deliverance, liberation; solutions to their problems were given and that made them climb ladders of higher heights today.

This book is a solution book, unlike lots of prayer book you might have come across all the times. This is a direct reciprocal of solutions to govern and usher, you to your purpose destined life on this earth. Read with all understanding and faith. As a result of spirit and revelation, you shall experience him mightily, so strong as you read along with a practical recognition of encounters in his presence. I hereby encourage you that you open up your heart, your spirit for Lord to set in to open the eyes of your understanding as you read this book from start to finish. Whatever problem, situation, desire will be answered in Jesus name. By the power, in the blood, I cast fear out of you to pave way for the Lord's visits because he will surely you read through this miracle book of the Lord called the other side of prayer. God wants to visits you so please allow him today. Prepare for the Lord's visitation now!!!!!

Confession

An Exaltation of prayer to the Lord.

Father, you know everything I do, from far away you understand all my thoughts. You see me, whether I am working or resting, you know all my actions, father even before I speak, you already know what I will say. You are all around me on every side. You protect me with your power. Your knowledge of me is too deep; it is beyond my understanding.

Where could I go to escape from you? Lord? Where could I get away from your presence? If I went up to heaven, you would be there; If I lay down in the world of the dead, you would be there. If I flew away beyond the east, north, south, west, or lived in the farthest place you would be there, to lead me. I could ask the darkness is not dark for you, and the night is a bright as the day. Darkness and light are the same to you.

You created every part of me; you put me together in my mother's womb. I praise you because you are to be praised and feared; All you do is strange and mighty, so wonderful I know it all with all of my heart. When my bones were being formed, carefully put together in my mother's womb, when I was growing there in the secret, you knew that I was there, you knew that I existed. You saw me before I was born. The days allotted to me had all been recorded in your book, before any of them ever begun.

O God, how difficult I find your thoughts. How many of them there are! If I counted them, they would be more than, the grains of sand. When I awake, I am still with you. O God, how I wish you would kill the wicked. How I wish violent people would leave me alone!

They say wicked things about you; they speak evil things against your name. O Lord examines me, O God of Abraham, Isaac, Jacob and knows my mind. test me and discover my thoughts. Find out if there is any evil in me and guide me in an everlasting way. Henceforth I decree this prayer answered in the name of Jesus!!! As you complete this prayer book my Lord our God will battle for you, and grant unto you every need, desire, every step of the way in Jesus name Amen.

Chapter One

An Argument For Prayer

Never see yourself just merely existing and carrying the load of everything towards the finishing line but there's no power in just existing. Today allow your soul rise for a new phase.

In Jobs uttermost extremely, he cried after the lord. Job 23:3,4.
"On that, I knew where I might find him; that I might come even to his seat! I would order my cause before him, and till my mouth with argument".

The longing desire of an afflicted child of God is once more to see his father's face. His first prayer is not oh that I might be healed, or see my children restored from the jaws of the grave, and my property once more restored alive from the hand of the spoiler; But the first and uppermost cry is 'oh that I knew where I might find him_ who is my God, that I might come even to his seat. God's children run home when the storm comes on. It is the heaven-born instinct of a gracious soul to seek shelter of safety and regained blessings beneath the wings of Jehovah.

It is further observable that though a good man hastens to God in his trouble and runs with all the more speed because of the unkindness of his fellow men, yet sometimes the gracious soul is left without the comfortable presence of God. This is the worse of all grieves. This is one of Job deep groans for deeper than any which came from him on an account of the loss of his children and his property; "Oh that I knew where I might find HIM". The worst of all losses is to lose the smile of God. He now had a foretaste of the bitterness of his redeemers cry, my God, my God, why hast thou forsaken me? In this later verse, Job teaches us how he meant to plead and intercede with God. He does, as it revealed the secret of his closet, and unveils the art of prayer. We are here admitted into the guild of suppliants; we are shown the art and mystery of pleading. We have thought to us the blessed handicraft and science of prayer and if we can be bound apprentice of Job's master we may acquire no little skill in interceding with God.

The next part of the argument of prayer is filling the mouth with an argument not filling the mouth word nor phrase nor pretty expressions, but filling the mouth with argument are the knocks of the rapper by which the gate is.

The other question is why are arguments to be used at all? The reply is certainly not because God is slow to give.

- Not because we can change the divine purpose
- Not because God needed to be informed of any

circumstance with regard to ourselves or of anything in connection with the mercy asked; the arguments to be used are for our own benefit, not for his. He requires of us to plead with him and to bring forth our strong reason as Isaiah saith because this will show that we feel the value of mercy. When a man searches for arguments for a thing it is because he attaches importance to that which he seeking.

Again, our use of arguments teaches us the ground upon which we obtain the blessing. If a man should come with the argument of his own merit, he would never succeed. The successful argument is always founded upon grace and hence the soul so pleading is made to understand intensely that it is by his grace and by grace alone that a sinner obtained anything of the Lord. Besides the use of argument is intended to still up to our fervency. The best prayers I have heard have been full of arguments. Sometimes my soul has been fairly melted down when I have listened to brethren who have come before God feeling the mercy to be really needed and that they must have it, for they, have awakened for fervency of the entire assembly. There no need of prayer at all as far as God is concerned but what a need of prayer. There no need of prayer at all as far as God is concerned but what a need there is for it on our own account! If we were not constrained to pray, I question whether we could even live as

Christians. So now we get two blessing. A blessing is the obtaining and a blessing in the seeking. The very act of prayer is a blessing.

To pray is as to bathe one's self in a purling stream, and to escape from the heart. To pray is to mount on eagle wings above the clouds and get into the clear heaven where God dwelleth.
To pray is to grasp heaven in one's body made a temple of the Holy Ghost. To pray is to enter the treasure house of God and to enrich one's self out of an inexhaustible storehouse. To pray is to grasp heaven in one's arms to embrace the deity within one's soul and feels one's body made a temple of the Holy Ghost.Apart from the answer, prayer is in itself a benediction. To pray my brethren is to cast off your burdens. It is to tear away your rags. To shake off diseases, curses, To pray is to fill with vision It is to reach the highest point of Christian health.

God gave us much to be in the Holy art of argument with HIM in prayer. It is well in prayer to plead with Jehovah his attributes. Abraham did so when he laid hold upon God's Justice. Sodom was to be pleaded for, and Abraham begins peradventure there be fifty righteous within the city; wilt thou also destroys and not spare the place. For the fifty righteous those are in there? Here it was a powerful argument by which the patriarch grasped the Lord's left hand, and arrested it just when the thunderbolt was about to fall. I may take hold at any time upon the Justice the mercy, wisdom, longsuffering tenderness of God and we shall find every attribute of the most high to be as it were, a great battering-ram, with which we may open the gates of heaven. Remember thou saith, surely I will do thee good, oh the force of that plea!!!. This is holding God to his words. This attribute is a splendid horn of the altar to lay hold upon but the promise which has in it the attributes and sometimes more is yet a mightier holdfast. Remember how David put it" thou sadist" after Nathan had spoken the promise David said at the close of his prayer do as thou has said, and shall he not do it? Let God be true. Let every man be a liar" shall he not keep his word? Solomon at the opening of the temple pleads with God to remember the promise. he promised his father David and to bless that place.

The third argument of prayer is using our own unworthiness as an argument with God" out of the eater comes forth meat and out of the strong comes forth sweetness. David in one place pleads thus; " Lord have mercy upon mine iniquity for it is great" that is a very singular mood of reasoning but being interpreted it means, Lord why. Shouldest thou go about doing little things? The power with which God restrains himself is great indeed. Brothers and sisters, there's such a thing as creeping down at the foot of the throne, crouching low and crying "O God break me not- I am bruised reed. Oh! Tread not on my little life. There was once an occasion when the very three Godhead of Jehovah made trumpet plea for the prophet Elijah. on that season when he had bidden his adversaries see whether God could answer them by fire, you can little guess the excitement there must have been that day in the prophets mind cry aloud for he is a god, either he is talking or he is pursuing, or he is on a journey or peradventure he sleepeth and must be awakened" and as they cut themselves with knives and leaped upon the altar, oh the scorn with which that man of God must have looked down upon their impotent exertions, and their earnest but useless cries! But think of how his heart must have palpitated if it had not been for the strength of his faith when he repaired the altar of God that was broken down and laid the wood in order; and killed the bullock. Hear him cry" pour out water on it. You shall not suspect me of concealing fire. He bids them do again for the three time, and when it was covered and fully soaked with water saturating through, then he stood up and cried to God, let it be known that thou only art God" here everything was put to test. Jehovah 's own existence was now put as it were stake; before the eyes of men by this bold prophet . down came the fire and devoured not only the sacrifice but also the wood, stones, even the water that was in the trenches.

For Jehovah God had answered prayer. We sometimes may do the same and say unto him and God shall show himself strong in our Rag situation and deal with the root of its existence. If you need anything of God asks. Virtually Jesus Christ says to us " If you need anything of God, all that the father has belongs to him.

So go and use his name. If ye ask anything in his name he will do it. There's no need to speak with fear and trembling or with bated breath. Waiver not and let not faith stagger. If thou pleads the name of Christ thou pleads that which shakes the gate of hell, and which the host of heaven obey and God himself feels the sacred power of that divine plea. Brethren you would do better if you sometimes through more in your prayers of Christ grief and groans. Bring before the Lord his wounds. Make the groan of Jesus cry again and
again in Gethsemane and his blood speaks again from that frozen Calvary. Speak out and tell the Lord that which is tormenting you today with such grief and cries groans to plead thou cannot take a denial. Such argument as these will speed you.

The fourth argument of prayer is when the Holy Ghost fills our mouth with argument and order our cause. The result is always as this, "we shall fill our mouth with praise in the end; victory" A man who has his mouth full of prayer will always have room for nothing else. Then come with this blessed mouthful and you shall so go way with whatever you asked God so delight thyself in him and he will give thee the desires of your heart. "Open your mouth wide and I shall fill it. God give you the force of it and to thy in humble prayer to the Lord Jesus Christ and to find eternal life in him.

Unaware Spirits

There is a real war in the world today. The battleground is in our homes and taken our children, most relatives captive. Jesus said a man's enemy are members of his household "Mathew 10:36"

- Just because you chose not to believe in the attachment of dark force and spirit does not mean that you or any other close cannot pick them up. Never deny the existence of spirits believe their existence, if not you will ultimately end up living your entire life with them. These spirits are not a belief; they are a simple fact of life. People who decide to deny their existence themselves always have the most problems because they are completely clueless as to what is really going on with themselves and their world around them. These also make their spiritual level challenged.

- Also keep in mind that there are demons, dark spirits, and angels, there are also god's .should somebody tells you these are false, tell them they don't exist in this world either beyond this physical dimension of life on earth there are beings which are non-physical, which are both dark and light. A human being who cannot see beyond the physical dimension are actually trapped on a consciousness level. This makes them scale themselves able to see small parts of life, thinking that small part of their life is all that exists. Listen to this, supposing you find yourself in this town or village where there are no television, cars schools, better jobs, no technology, should you live there all your life. You would believe strongly that whatever you find in that town or village your entire life is all that matters to you. I tell you this makes you limited. Very similar to this story is the dimension of physical and non- physical life. People who have not gone beyond the physical dimension are trapped within it and are trained to believe that it is all that exists. God doesn't have limited resources. He blesses that no one can curse.

- Only atheists, non-religious people or sinners can pick up spirit and demon/dark forces this is false. All people can pick up spirits and demons regardless of age, sex, intelligence level, religious preference, financial status, personality, hair color etc. This is a made up religious belief created to keep people who believe it trapped in the belief and unaware of truth .know what around and pray to tackle right from the roots of it with the knowledge to break through fully. Understand what you dealing with. Understand what has fighting you. no need praying amiss. That all this book is about. THE OTHER SIDE OF PRAYER. Bible says we wrestle not against flesh and blood but against principalities, against powers against rulers of the darkness of this world, against spiritual wickedness in high place "Eph 6:12"

- Spirit and demons one may say can be removed or dealt with, with spells, chanting/mantras, sound, salt, magic sorcery, cleansing, white light. This is false.

Believe that when the spirit or dark entities decides to attach itself to you or anyone else it is not going to leave without being forced by PRAYER. Some spirits of these spirits even decide to hunt and torment you right from the day you were born until you die. So until you come out of your shell with the action of prayer in the word, there is no way it will leave. it won't just go anywhere. They are always moved out of people and mediums by some force that is greater than them. That force of power is what I share with you today Jesus, the word. At the mentioning of this name every knee must bow, every tongue confesses that indeed YES he is. All principalities, power, rulers of this dark are fear. Now notice that in this world anything is difficult when you lack the right tool to use. Keep this in mind casting out or removing these spirits unaware can never be done well by these methods such as sacrifices to gods, animals, chanting etc. by most occultist, spiritualists,

psychics/ mediums, even false prophets because they all consult same demonic powers and spirit, they operate with.
All these can be dealt with properly through prayer. Prayer based on the word and power of the holy ghost, the name and the blood of Jesus.

- Demons, spirits, and dark force are something you should fear. This is also false; these force of darkness are not to be feared." Remember we are not given the spirit of fear and timidity but of power, love, and self-discipline. 2Timothy 1:7". Instead, they are something that we need to understand that they exist. Also, fear itself is a spirit which is not of God. The moment you fear them, then you have chosen to give them the power to react over you. If you fear them, then you have not learned how to deal with them; failing to deal with them only makes you fear them more. What you hide from and deny only creates a bigger more powerful form of fear.

- You have to be trained to remove spirits, demons or dark force. This is also false. The moment you accept Christ he becomes your salvation. He lives in you as you abide in him, he gives you power. Notice his should a Christian not yet an unbeliever can only believe this name Jesus and get saved anytime he /she is attacked how much more you who is saved. Spirits are mostly interested in using people. These dark force are interested in stealing people's joy and power.

- Have you to be hearing voices to crazy or possessed before you will know spirit exist? This is false. You do not have to be possessed before you know they surely exist. There's no need allowing yourself to be on that level before you know you are fully possessed. Some persons are working, still functioning, have good friends, do all normal things yet get possessed. These are spirit and forces everywhere all around us unaware.

How will you know you attached with some of these spirits and demons around you? Certain lifestyles will determine whether you are demon possessed or not. One thing we should know is that the prince of the world is already here with us "the thief cometh to steal, kill and destroy". Until he has something of his in you, he can never get attached to you. Most life styles which bible speaks against that is practiced in today world determine if a person is possessed or not. Most of such practical and lifestyles can be seen the book of Romans Chapter 1'.

Most of these practices are introduced to the youth of today from families, through schools, occultic groups, and societies. With time these attract spirits that set in to destroy human lives. My brothers and sisters, I just want you to know in all these, God is the greatest of all these things. What shall we say to these(evil) things? If God be for us then who shall be against us? If in Greek means since!!! So since God is for us .... We conquer. Still, I believe the most powerful thing is the presence of GOD. Know him now and he shall set you free from all these. As Jesus commanded those demons out if that man "luke 4:33-36".

In the synagogue was a man who had the spirit of a demon in him, he screamed out loud voice, "ah! What do you want with us, Jesus of Nazareth? Are you here to destroy us? I know who you; you are God's holy messenger immediately Jesus ordered the spirit, "be quiet and come out of him! The demons threw the man in front of them and went out of him. The people were all amazed and said to one another,"

What kind of words are these? With authority and power, this man Jesus of Nazareth gives orders to the evil spirit and demons and they come out. They obey Him. Except this name my brethren I confess in this book to you that;

- No salt
- No wine
- No water

Nothing without the presence of God moves anything permanently.

Be careful Around You

One may ask "are you deterring to people…… Judas ?well my answer stays YES!!! JUDAS is good for the destiny direction. If not for him we would still wonder if Jesus is the one was and is and is come. On the hand, we must avoid the DESTINY KILLERS.

The Bible warns us about satan and its precious possessed. Do you recognize Satan greater deception and how to avoid them? Our world today is filled with liars and thieves, who seek to defraud us. The giant deceiver is with us today. The devil and his tactics. Are you prepared to avoid him after reading this book? Or would you fall a victim to his deceptive schemes?

Are you also aware that this thief works through deceptive practices, from selfish/ vanity to pride, dangerous occultism, seeking to turn people away from the truth and from the way of life that will bring true happiness in God's way to mankind. Many of you who read this book will be alive during that traumatic time when the devil takes place fully in the very future near, Called the new age Note this, the great dragon was cast out, that serpent of old the devil. Satan is here with us and so are his angles (Rev.12:9) just imagine thieves breaking into your home and robbing you of your possessions do not think because you are a religious person, man or woman of god , believer, a child of god you can not be deceived? Jesus revealed that one of the most pervasive forms of deception is found in religious practice. Apostle Paul warns the Corinthians against false ministers; for such are false apostles, deceitful workers, transforming themselves into apostles, prophets, and workers of Christ Jesus. The devil has lots of schemes and devices to deceive us Christians should recognize Blatant satanic influence.

Again we say be careful; we lock our doors but how do we protect ourselves from the spiritual attacks? Many such spiritual attacks manifest physically in setbacks, delays, stagnation, promise and fail disappointment etc. Many of such also do manifest in marital problems and causing break-ups or separations. While you want your revenge on your enemies, you should still rather get your goods stolen restored. How do we channel our energy onto the restoration over the vengeance? We know that in all things god works together for our good with those who love him, those whom he has called according to his purpose "Romans 8:28". This is the truth!! Now again how can you tell truth from error? Bible gives us again answer, as Jesus prayed concerning his disciples" sanctify them by truth". Your words are the truth(john 17:17). Yet satan can still deceive religious people. He appears deceptively as an angel of light using counterfeit people who appear innocent, crafty but actually fraudulent deceivers. As Christians, we need to be aware of all these. These ruin lots of destinies and marriages as result of making the massive wrong choice. So sad that in our world today majority will not want to hear the truth. Most chasing signs and wonder." All these shall pass away but this words shall remain forever. Don't forget in the book of Samuel gods spirit left Saul though he still ruled as a king of Israel until Samuel received confirmation from God to the house of jersey to anoint David as the next king of Israel. You could realize the evil spirit then got closer to Saul. The same is happening around us today.

Christians are shifting their faith in god to one-sided part called miracles, signs, wonders living the truth in his words . all these are errors in the Christendom. Most of these leaders are shifting yet operating in their gifts. Never forget that gift according to the bible are without repentance. So most may still be operating in them yet not backed by the spirit and presence of Christ the living lord. Another deception of the enemy is, he seeks for teachers to teach their own words. Instead of the truth in the bible. Apostle Paul exhorted TIMOTHY Preach the word; be careful in season and out of season. convince, Rebuke, exhort. With all longsuffering and teaching, for a time will come when they will not endure sound doctrine but according to their own idea".

The book of Jude talks much about deception in our world today. People in wolves in sheep clothing. Don't be shaken by their face and names. Only the voice of God. Are you now willing to be guided and corrected by the BIBLE? !!! OR will you be turned aside to tables?

Let's not forget that cultures are also a contributory factor to deception and counterfeit practices. Remember Jesus warming the Pharisees and scribes concerning certain religious practices and traditions against the commandment of god .the book of revelation also warn us about pervasive deception. " rev. 6:2" for many will come in my name as the Christ and will deceive many(math. 24:5-5).

Lust

Human nature is filled with vanity, jealousy, greed, lust. Santa can take advantage of that tendency and weakness in all of us. He sends temptations through the media, television, magazines, people with canal picture on these. Verse 9 down till end please read.

Pride; Vanity and Arrogance

God opposes the proud but gives grace to while pride harms only the proud, arrogance due to overbearing pride brings contempt for others. An arrogant person is often rude and fond of offending his friend, relative colleagues and everyone else who comes in contact with him. Often people are confused between various terms associated with pride. An attempt to show the difference between them and how to control them.

Pride

Pride rears its head even in the most unsuspected corners one may be proud that he is proud, another proud that he is not proud. While one may proud that he is a non-believer in god, another may be proud of his devoting to god. Learning may render one man proud, and yet ignorance can also be a source of pride for another man.

Vanity

Another by- product of pride is vanity, which intensely craves admiration and applause. It is an undue assumption of self-importance. It often results in open and rude expression of contempt and hostility .it quickly takes for granted superiority and privilege, which other are slow to concede.

Arrogance

An absorbing sense of once own greatness. It is a feeling of one's superiority over others. In the presence of superiors, over weeping pride manifest itself as arrogance. Pride is too self-satisfied to care for seeing the good in others and in praising them.

Scriptural Reference

JAMES 4:6, , Isaiah 2:11, chronicles 26:16 Psalm 10:3-4 Psalm 59:12, Prov 6:16-19, math.4:8-9. Selfishness and egotism are also a part and parcel of human nature. Most people like to feel important. The Apostles Paul introduces timothy concerning the ordination as a bishop or an overseer. He wrote that such a candidate should be not novice lest being puffed up with pride he fall into the same condemnation as the devil. Moreover, he should have a good testimony around the outside (Tim 3:6-7). Do you allow pride, vanity guide your thinking and behavior?

Remember few biblical example of people who fell victim to these. Lucifer the devil once tried to challenge the authority of god out pride was down unto this earth. Remember Ananias and sapphire in act 5" Remember Saul then later Paul the apostle on his way to Damascus.

Lying

(Act 5:1-5) Ananias and sapphire. Is even parts of the commandment of God. Lies are deliberately untruthful, false accusations, deceitful reports people today fabricate stories, lies to mislead people to accept than to accept the truth. This is misleading the church, and also sinning against the father, son, holy spirit. This is also a fool of the growing so much in our dispensation today. People everywhere are lying for all they wish for. Also at the heart of all sin is a lie.

Bitterness

Getting disappointed by others is painful. But allowing the hurt to germinate in your heart makes you bitter. It makes you replay all the time your heart and blocks you from progressing. It makes you all the time angry ever over issues that you need to laugh over, Rom 12:18 says "if is possible as far as it depends on you, live at peace with everyone. Let's know that God requires forgiveness Eph 4:32" he shall judge us all in the end accordingly. Understand that no matter what goes on, we are forgiven as the forgives us.

Lack of Faith

This is a sin. This is a reason why so may Christians today struggle. "Heb 3:8". Confess positively with your mouth. There's power in your tongue (life and death). Nothing exposes our sinfulness like the word of God. It blows away the thick fog of deception and lets us see sin for what it really is. Not that we allow in it but that might flee from it. Remember the promise concerning the power of Gods word in Hebrew 4:12-13 devil, therefore, my goal today is to let the word show us what sin is, and why it is sin. God diagnosis of our human disease called sin. I offer to you today best physician, a sin Specialist and his medicine which is needed to keep the disease(sin) in check. The medicine is the word and he is the word. He is Jesus.

Voice of the Blood

But for a time I was just there……….. surviving, not really applying the real energy that is required for victory. I was just a survival mode. But today, I have a rejuvenating power " to God be the glory " He proves that he can help us by the BLOOD. Ephesians 2:13

Blood in Greek called (HAIMA) is the most costly sacrifice in the old testament. Can you imagine how many priests it took only in a day to slaughter 22,000 oxen, 120,000 sheep as a sacrifice to the lord in just a day by Solomon? You realized it cost Solomon lot of sacrifice to offer many animals. Now how much the father in heaven. It took HIM his son. His only begotten not made by man but father his only beloved son and king." Act 20:28". He purchased us with the blood of the lamb. It cost him so much to be precise everything for that sacrifice on Calvary's CROSS. Where the blood of Jesus was shed. Imagine the trace of blood right from
the Old Testament to new where blood was shed. It was seven times" you noticed the every man is the bible who built an altar and applies the blood right from Abraham- Isaac- Jacob and the rest understood the blood covenant. As you know god is a covenant keeping god. "Job 1:9- 10". Anytime the blood is applied the anointing follows. What does the blood of Jesus actually do?

Mercy, not sacrifice. A basic principle of Christianity is that Jesus Christ died on the cross for our sins. What exactly this means has increasingly come under debate in recent time. In these times people have understood" this penal substitution". Again most attributed the death as an assumption that primary problem resolved by the cross is gods anger about our sin. Now these are two separate issues. I believe "penal substitution" has biblical support but it has been drastically over weighted. I also do not believe that a view of the cross is an appeasement of god anger; biblically faithful. One way of this phenomenon is to look at all the reference to Jesus blood in the new testament to see what the bible says that the blood actually does. The blood establishes a new covenant “mark 14:24” Jesus said this is my blood which is poured out of many. My blood which seals god's covenant amen

- Again in Luke 22: 20, in the same way, he gave them the cup after the supper, saying this cup is god's new covenant sealed with my blood which is poured out of you!!!

- In Mathew 26: 28; this is my blood, which seals god's covenant, blood poured out for many for the forgiveness of sins. “ 1 Corinthians 11:25” in the same way, he took the cup after supper and said, this is god's new covenant, sealed with my blood. Whenever you drink it, do so in the memory of me”

In Romans 3:23-25” say' everyone has sinned and is far away from God's saving presence, but by the free gift of god's grace all are put right with him through Christ Jesus, who sets them free.

God offered him, so that by his blood, he should become the means by which people sins are forgiven through their faith in him. Again Hebrews 9:12” is when Christ went through the tent and entered once and for all into the holiest place”, he did not take the blood of goats and bulls to offer as a sacrifice, rather, he took his own blood and obtained eternal salvation for you and me. note the of goats and bulls and the ashes of a burnt calf are sprinkled on the people who are ritually unclear, and this purifies them by taking their rituals impurity. Since this Is true, how much more is accomplished by the blood of Christ Through the eternal spirit he offered himself as a perfect sacrifice to God. His blood will purify our conscience from useless rituals, so that we may serve the living god.

In Jesus words of institution for the lord's supper in Mathew, Mark, Luke as well quoted by Paul in 1corinthians he say's that his blood is the basis of for a new covenant. In Romans 3:24” there a Jewish ritual of “YOM KIPPUR” (THE DAY OF ATONEMENT) in which mercy seat of the Ark of the covenant is covered with the

blood of sacrificial bull as part of the official act by which Israel's covenant with god is restored after a years worth of sin. Heb 9:12 makes more explicitly in its reference to the holy holies where the priest would go on “Yom Kippur”. Jesus blood purifies us!!!
Heb 9:4-22, Heb 13:10-12.

We have an altar from which those who officiate in the tent have no right to eat, for the bodies of those animals whose blood is brought into the sanctuary by the high priest as a sacrifice for sin are burned outside the camp. Therefore Jesus also suffered outside the city gate in order to sanctify the people by his own blood. 1john 1:7, Rev7:14. I think that the cleansing function of Jesus blood gives us the most trouble as interpreters outside of pre-scientific context. For ancient people the blood of an unblemished animal was the cleanest and holiest thing you could possibly touch, Heb 9:19” for when every commandment had been told to all people by mosses in accordance with the law, he took the blood of calves and goats, with water and scarlet wool and hyssop and sprinkled booth the scroll itself and all the people. Lev 17:11, blood makes atonement as life. So as we are cleansed by the blood of Jesus, it not through feeling guilty about the contribution of our sins to the punishment of the cross. It is rather that his blood is a pure and holy source of life that cleanses us eternally, particularly through our sacramental ingestion of it in the wine that we share in holy Eucharist.

Take this from my brethren, like an attorney you must see the blood intercession as the grace of God on our behalf.John 3:16”

Don't Give Up The Beginning

Never give up your beginning; though beginning has always been difficult. They may ask questions as these –can you do it?

- Can you complete what you have just started?
- Are you sure? Your response should always be yes I can by FAITH. Personally, I don't at times get something right from the beginning. I get encouraged each time I try again and again.

Thanks to God Almighty and my mentor Apostle Dr. Denise Thorpe.She is such a great inspiration to my life. I always thank God for her life and family. Mom, Dad, Brother , Sister , some days seem harder than others. Mistakes seen magnified and insults cut a little deeper. Someday life is way too hard. On these days I once panicked until it felt like my anxiety would hold my spirit. Hostage forever, but through god healing grace and awareness to look for inspiring things to revise spirit, the shadows are beginning to give way to clarity, peace and the return of hope. also know that "salvation is progressive" 1peter 1:8-12. You love
him, although you have not seen him, and you believe in him although you do not see him. So you rejoice with a great and glorious joy which words cannot express because you are receiving the salvation of your souls. Which is the purpose of your faith in him? So the moment you get saved as you tell it, accept Christ, old things are passed away. You tell yourself and your spirit man inside you that you can you can do all things to prosper. 1phil 4:13" change your mentality. Your way of reasoning today. The mind is a footstool for the devil. Don't fall victim to his tricks and negative of failure. Active the power of faith in you today and say to yourself that indeed you can make it!!! You are making it!!! You shall make it!!! You will make it!!! Indeed all shall come to pass. Few reference scriptures

- Gen. 2:7 1Corin. 15:45" Matthew 10:39,
- Luke 9:25, 1Corin. 15:54 - 57 Rom. 2:7
- Rev. 2:11,20:6, 1 Peter 1:3, Heb. 11:6

Foundation in the word of God above every opinion of the man. If you are going to base your entire life on something. You want to know that it is solid then I recommend God's opinion in this word to you today. If you are going to take your whole life around or on that thing as so you can trust then let it be Christ the solid. Know Him in His word. He is the truth that sets free. It will be utterly tragic and disastrous to spend your entire life on a path that you thought led to heaven; only to find out it's too late after missing your path. Proverbs 14:12 says!! Don't allow man's opinion overshadows Gods word. A man may lead you to death. A man may

lead to destruction, a man may deceive you to shift your salvation. Man's opinion will always thwart God's purpose concerning your life. People can trick those who refuse to hear god for themselves. With their own knowledge and understanding, " proverb 3:5". Don't ever get too busy for God, are you? it's a prime danger for Christians today to get too busy for God to the extent of losing their spiritual focus. Especially as the pace of society hastens, this is a real danger to spiritual growth!!!.

Jesus Christ gave this warning to this last generation leading up to his second coming; it's worth taking heed, today". And to the angel of the church of the Laodicea's write these things say the Amen, faithful and true witness, the beginning of the creation of god. I know your works; that you are neither hot nor cold. I wish you were cold or hot.(Rev 3:14- 15). The condition of many just prior to his return- even many Christians will be profound complacency .they aren't necessary out in the would in
rebellion against him, but neither are they on fire for him and his work; they're just too busy with other things. Cares of the world are crowding out their relationship with God. Don't confess business with growth. If God has opened your mind to awesome truth and you've been called out of this world of chaos and confusion be grateful and grow today. No more you can't. No more quitting. Get involved in God's work. Never let busy-ness side track you from fulfilling your "ultimate destiny"

- The relationship has to be personal. Your relationship with God has to be you. know him yourself. A miracle without his word of prayer is baseless. He is the only key and way to life. No third party. No man can call God for you. Man can lead you to Christ but know him yourself as an individual. Carry your own cross. Fight your own salvation .no third party. A prophet or a man of god is good but they should not replace relationships with god. They are not and can't be God. They are men. Should you take off God they are dust like. Should you add God they become a man of God. They should only confirm what God said in the natural way, how God reveals to them only either good or bad and not adding or deducting. Mind you God doesn't speak all the time. God only speaks to those who love prayer much and build their relationship with him based on his prayer and his word. Are you ready now?

Here are few uplifting quotes that are like medicine for your soul.

1. A leap of faith" faith is taking the step even when you don't see the whole staircases. Stand in faith!! Walk by faith!! Live a life of faith!!
2. Around the roadblocks, most important things in this world have been accomplished by people who kept on trying when there seemed to be no hope of.
3. Spark your ignition. The decision is the spark that ignites action. Until a decision is made, nothing happens.
4. Never give up - when you feel like quitting, think about why you started.
5. Stay positive- the pessimist sees difficulty is every opportunity. The optimist sees the opportunity in every difficulty.
6. Light in darkness - hope is being able to see light in every darkness despite all odd.
7. Keep your dream alive - you are never too old to set another goal or dream. When you fall ten times. Do it again, again. Believe you can prevail.
8. Stay strong- don't give up the beginning. Is always the hardest suffering and is optional.
9. Pain is evitable.

CHAPTER TWO

Ask God what you do not know

Whether you've grown up warming church pews or avoiding church like the plague, chance is you'll face different challenges when it comes to growing your prayer life. And sometimes, even if you've been praying for sixty years or less, you may come to point where you feel like need to start all over again. " but that ok". Your path may seem a little different from mine. That's the beauty of having God as a solemn tutor. He personalizes our course work to fit each of unique spiritual needs when it seems difficult we still keep pressing on because we have this great promise. " the prayer of a righteous person is powerful and effective James 5:16". So now every child of God reading this book, the spirit that raised Jesus from the dead is alive in you, just waiting for you to reach out to him. As easier as a student, and you too can learn to pray.

1. Ask God to teach you how to pray!! Admit that you don't yet have the power to this fundamental Christian discipline like the disciples say 'Lord teaches us to pray' Luke 11:1. That the humbling prayer, and a courageous one us well. The great news is God will always answer that prayer. He answers. He is willing to take you deeper into the spirit of prayer to show you riches you even fathomed before.

2. Talk to God as your friend: All of us know at least one person who seems to adopt an entirely different person when they are praying, is the sound of their voice change and words of choice not sounding anything like their regular selves. That is not all that right. Be realistic and honest praying AS Jesus taught His disciples. Tell God the great news you would text a friend and thank him for making it happen. Talk to Him to about every tragic news received and ask him to help you. When you do this I tell you that anger, frustrations or doubt you may sometimes feel will all be cleared off. He is big enough to handle the good, bad, ugly.

3. Keep prayer journal: You can write down your prayers so that

your mind stays focused on the prayers and not on the things you need to do. Always enjoy reading what God did for people in the bible through answering prayer. Talk of Hannah, Jacob, Joseph, Ruth and Naomi, the woman with the issue of blood, so on.

4. Pray Bible prayers -: This is one of my experiences of growth in my prayer life as I started studying and praying Bible prayers. You realized it encourages and inspires you more. Few scripture references; Matt 6:9-13, John 17, Ephes. 3:16-21, Colos. 1: 9-14, Psalm 51, psalm 42, Psalm 35, Psalm 63. Many of these prayers are refreshing and are deep with rich meaning. As you read the Bible underline some key scriptures that get you in the mood to pattern the Lord.

5. Find a trusted and a reliable prayer partner: The deepest seasons of prayers have always been accompanied by praying with others. Jesus promises to show up in a two special ways when anytime two or three agree in prayer. In His name: Matt 18:20. That a reason enough to get into prayer with a partner. There is power in praying together. Remember the walls of Jericho.

6. Become a lifelong learner- guide yourself against spiritual pride that draws our attention god to ourselves. Always keep asking god to teach you what you do not know more and more each day. scripture Jeremiah 33, John 15, Matthew 5

He walks beside you

Is the one beside you Jesus? Is he the man you call a friend? Is he friendly? Anyways green is my favorite color!!! I don't know about you.

- Green because makes it fruitful. Green because is in motion. Always at work and so is my Jesus. When He's with you, you not alone. He's always with you as a tree planted by the rivers of living waters. Your green never dries up. It neither withers.

  He walks beside with peter on the stormy sea. He walks beside you and will guide you.

  He shall show you the way for he is the way, the truth, and life. He's green to me. When I am lost He knows where am going. When am Confused within my mind, He understands and I know He does. When I am tired and feel that I just can't go on that's when He encourages me that I can. I am not a failure.

- When am wrong He corrects me. He always makes it right.

- When am cold I feel His warmth around me When am blind to other needs He point them out to me, and He leads on before me.

Is Anyone Listening

Have you ever been in a meeting or a group discussion and wondered if the other person was really listening to you whiles you talk? Most people take their listening skills for granted we often feel and know we have the listening skill and that others know they are being heard. But we leaders struggle with tasks and roles that directly relate to listening. Accepting criticism. Well/ dealing with people's feelings and trying to understand what other think all require good listening skills and a good listener. Only Jesus Christ is the best listener.

- He doesn't give you a hard time concentrating on what makes you sad, he rather listens and encourages you.

- He's not worried about t say next rather he tells you what to say as your speaker.

- He doesn't question someone ideas or actions. He doesn't dislike opinions. He listens to all.

- He gives advice too soon and suggests solutions to problems before it even happens.

- He talks significantly so well with all.

- Pay attention to what he says in his words. Be ok with silence. Is most in these times He visits and performs miracles.
- He encourages people to offer idea and solutions before He seal to perfection.

- He helps you fight your freedom through his blood.

- He is your past, present, future. He went with the Israelites, out of Egypt through the red sea to their promised land. He shall do same for you today now and forever. Makes him your lord.

Love Heard My Plead

Psalm 116: “1” 6: 9”
The Lord heard my voice, my cry for mercy He accept my prayer. Psalm 6: 8-10 again the psalmist David having made his request known to God, He is confident that his sorrow will be turned into joy. By the workings of God's grace upon His heart, he knows is prayer was accepted and did not doubt but it in due time, be answered. His prayers will be accepted coming out of the hands of Christ the mediator. The word signifies prayer made to God of His righteousness who will plead His cause and write His wrongs. A believer, through the blood and righteousness of Christ, can go to God as a righteous God and plead with Him for pardon and cleansing, who is just and faithful to grant both except Christ. He prays for the conversion of his enemies or foretells their ruin. In 1samuel 1:”27” For this boy I prayed and Lord has given me my petition which I ask of Him. Though God works with season and time but as with these He always answers prayer. H e shall answer u today. Talk to Him all with all concerns, every heart desire, and He shall surely answer. Has He said and would not do? He said come to Him all ye that labor and He shall give you rest. I don't know what you going through today. I don't know your struggle and troubles your false stigma or label I encourage you now that all is not lost. All is not gone yet. Trust in Jesus, the anther and finisher of our faith. He's right here and now. Talk to Him, All is in Him. He will answer. Just a prayer ahead. Pray now Brethren.

Worship Him now!!

Before the throne of God Above”
I have a strong and perfect plea.
Great high priesthood whose home is love.
Who ever lives and pleads for me.
His name is greater on His Hands.
My name is written on His heart.
I know that while in heaven He stand, No tongue can bid me thence depart”

- When satan bids me to despair And tells me of guilt within, upward. I look and see him there, who made an end to all my sin. Because a sinless savior died. My sinful soul is counted free. For god the trust is satisfied. To look on him and pardoned me.

- Behold him there the risen lamb

My perfect, spotless righteousness. The great unsearchable I AM, the king of glory and of grace. One in himself cannot die. My soul is purchased by his blood. My life is hidden with Christ on high, with Christ my savior and my God Amen.

CHAPTER THREE

It Puts You In Chase

Your existence is not a mistake, neither is a problem unsolved or a problem to chase you to death. Your existence is not a burden or an inconvenience. Your existence can never be a nuisance to society if you allow Gods lead. Your existence again is a gift of God, a miracle in his sight to many. God knows how long you have waited.

I assure you that every second of it all will be worth going through in the end, for his glory to be fulfilled in your life. God has used for all of us here on earth. Never settle for the mediocrity of a religious life. Shake your world around you with prayer, wisdom boldness, and freedom. Stand strong in the middle of the road as fulfill your God-given destiny and calling. The journey wouldn't be easy then as the promised, but with him, we shall push through successfully. Whatever that's going wrong in your life today shouldn't push you in chase brethren.

There's nothing God can't do or through prayer. Don't be dismayed to be chased off your faith in he always catches us when we fall or teaches us how to fly. Prayer is the only fuel of our faith with the story of Hannah in "1 Samuel 9-18"

"Hannah was chased in desperation for her inability of childbirth. She was barren after married for years. Her rival peninnar had children. Bible said one day after they had finished their meal in the house of the Lord at Shiloh, Hanner goes up. She was deeply distressed, and she cried bitterly as she prayed to the Lord.Hannah made a solemn promise to the Lord as his servant". Hannah asked God to see her troubled and remember her. She prayed her heart out so deep to the Lord for only just a son. She continued to pray for long. You realized she was very troubled and heartbroken. She felt so miserable. Until her situation put her in chase to seek God diligently her prays was answered. At times in life dreadful situation come our way that seems to tear us apart. I believe in seeking God almost all my time. Let's not wait until we trouble and chased by their same trouble before we seek God. Bible says in Hebrews 11:6" explains.

Wipe Out Mans Destiny

I' am fascinated that the very one who claimed he could forgive people sins (math 9:6) the very onc who insisted, he had a timeless nature john 8:58, the very one who exhibited (math 9:4), Luke 11:7 is seen engaging repeated in one of the most fundamental exercises of dependence. That's PRAYER.

We know there are lots happening with and around us, challenged situations and negative words and acts of the people we sometimes put our trust in try to deform us and ride us off our destiny's, I've realized personally that most of those problems such as false and confused confession and prophecies that some people, some men, and women of God try to use all in the of God do wipe out destinies. Most do those out of their selfish gains, others too are just agents from the pit of hell to destroy God's children. Spiritual robbers. Others are false medical reports. You noticed in our hospitals today most medical precautions and results are just false though am not disputing the fact that there aren't good reports sure there are. Medicine is good as seeking medical attention.

It becomes deadly and evil when these medical soldiers seek only interested in money than saving lives. Others accept a contract to inject false reports that drain lives at the edge of killing them inside. We should realize we are in the end time and everything bible talks about is true, and is happening each day. I just want you the reader to know how impartial It is to pray every second, minutes, hour about everything, as to step out of your room secured each day, it takes grace. Some people are so mean that there's nothing good in their blood, no matter who you are what you do or become, the moment they see your star right from the day you are born, they only keep pursuing your life and rob you of your destiny.

Until you know God to realize these negatives and mount on prayer to overcome them, you shall never enjoy the glory of God.

My Little Counts

A couple of days ago, I was talking about failure, and how it affects people. Some will set the bar too high, then fail and give up. I don't really mind failing. I've had my fair share of it and my fair share of success. Why? Because when I failed, I never give up. I kept going. Every little bit helps. Any contribution can be useful, as he can only give us one day, but every little bit helps, save money, save time, save energy.

I don't know why but these two ideas seem to be at odds with each other: money and ministry. Being a Christian is wealth. Jesus is never poor. If you make too much money or have nice material possessions, you're probably not serving Jesus. If you are voluntarily poor and minimalist, you're probably liking the gospel at least that's what we perceive.

It's a tension we don't bring up often. But it's a conversation I want to have with you. I guarantee you it will be worth it. My passion is I do long to see. Worship leader, church planter, pastors, apostolic leaders released to do the work of the ministry so well in their generation. I long to see the lost saved, the sick healed the gospel proclaimed to all the unreached people groups. I want to spend my life raising up leaders who will be so close to the presence of God, ushering the church into deeper levels of his presence. But there's a story I hear more often, a story most of us ministers are afraid to tell about ministry.

It Is good to work or do business for a living.Is also good to be into ministry all alone. I realized each one of us acquires certain skill before ministry based on gifts and talents deposited in us by God. Most trade upon such talents through education before ministry. These shouldn't end there. After entering into ministry, occupation is very good you noticed in the life of Jesus he went through some sort of vocation based on His father's work. In our world, today is one-sided move. You acquire skills and knowledge with which u can impart into others in ministry. Yet most bury these skills, instead rely solely on the members and church coffers for a living. Most don't impart. Most lack giving and sowing of seed and payment of tithes just as their encourage members to pay theirs. I tell is worth for every minister and member to pay tithe and contribute to the kingdom of God. Is also necessary sowing with our little of every knowledge we have acquired into ministry. My little count and so is yours. All it takes is the heart towards that worthy cause.

Remember the shunamite widow and Elisha in 2kings 4:1 - 38, whatever a man soweth so shall he reap

“Galatians 6:7” Elijah and the widow from Zarephath. You could see after this prophet received they give back their little through prayer for miracles to take place. In this our dispensation, majority are only into trickery deceiving the church only giving. No one gives just for giving sake. People give generously to receive.

There's no need playing tricks on God people as they. Everyone needs to contribute his or her little of whatever you have made.

I Deserve Everything

I asked for everything I deserve but I don't deserve everything I don't ask for. Most people who mean everything they say, get everything they ask for with faith. You own everything that happens to you if you not walking on the path of righteousness. You will then need to tell your story or write them. Is always worth to behave better to enjoy good things in life. We should also have in mind that whatever we doing now we shall account for either good or bad. This determines our outcome. If you love two things at the same time and choose the second, what happens to the first love?

For God so loved the world that He gave his only begotten son that whosever believes in him should not perish but have everlasting life. "john 3:16.

Everything is hard before it becomes easy. Mathew 6:33 says, seek ye first, the kingdom o God and all other things shall be added unto you. After knowing him, he gives you everything you deserve permanently without any sorrow. Narrow is the way for those who seek first the kingdom of God. Seek him first to know all right paths to life that saves your soul. With this, you can never be deceived or disappointed.The rest of everything after enjoying we leave them behind. It's always been worth seeking the things of God first then the worlds. Primarily we deserve the salvation that is in the kingdom of God because it is a greater value than all the world's riches.Does This mean that we should neglect the reasonable and daily duties that help sustain our lives? Certainly not. But as a Christian, there should be a difference in attitude toward them. If we are taking care of God's business as a priority seeking his salvation, living in obedience to him and sharing the good news of the kingdom with others, then he will take care of us as he promised and if that's the arrangement where is worrying? But how do we know if truly we seeking God's kingdom first? Few questions come to mind. Where do I primarily spend my energies? Is all my time and money spent on goods and activities that will certainly perish, or in the service of God?

The results of which I live is for eternity. God has promised to provide for his own supplying every need(Philip 4:19) but his idea of what we need basically has always been different from ours, and his timing will only occasionally meet our expectations. Example; most of our needs maybe riches or advancement but perhaps God knows what we truly do not need is poverty, loss or solitude. When this happens, we are in good company. God loved both Job and Elijah (Job 1-2;1 kings 18-19) in both cases, God followed these trials with restoration and sustenance. Don't follow these negative one way preaching that's all on the run in our world today that there's no suffering in Christianity but only need to be rich at all cost. I call it the prosperity gospel, that is making the most shift from the truth. This philosophy is not the counsel of the bible, and certainly not " Mathew 6:33" which is not a formula for gaining wealth but a description of how God works.

CHAPTER FOUR

The Fire In You, The Fire In Me

The fire that burns in your soul helps to sustain you through difficult times. This fire creates the energy necessary to overcome obstacles and solve problems. It also creates the momentum to take you closer to realizing your dreams.Sometimes the fire that fuels your passion to pray can flicker and burn out, with no flame to show you the way. Christ in you, is the hope of glory Colossians 1:27 your relationship with the father and knowing him in his word keeps igniting the fire in you. He is in you, you in him. This makes you pray so deeper into realms that keep your surrounding to a shake full of fire and flames. It makes you experience the real burning sensation of the Holy Ghost power, around you. Acts chapter2" on the day of Pentecost" the believers were gathered together in one place; Suddenly there was a noise from the sky which sounded like a strong wind blowing and it filled the whole house where they were sitting. Then they saw like tongues of fire which spread out and touched each person there. They were all filled with the Holy Spirit and began to talk in other languages, as the spirit enabled them to speak. These are few scripture references that talks much about the Holy Spirit and its works. Acts 10:38, Luke 4:18-19, Mathew 1:35. You could also realize in life that with no flame you may begin to feel hopeless and feel like giving for you. as a Christian, your fire should speak for you. it should fuel your miracle and shake the kingdoms of hell anytime you pray. Either than that you become an empty tool to the devil. That when most Christians then turn to Broadway. The way that leads to destruction.desire for holy ghost baptism today and now if you don't have it. Is so amazing that he becomes your teacher. Your advocator your peace. He becomes the prime key to your destiny. He becomes your companion, your compassion. He becomes your life and everything. The following ways are also a guide to reignite your fire inside you, the fuel needed to go again in life to achieve a life filled with happiness.

1. ***Your commitment:***

Are you human doing or you want without allowing anything get your way. Setbacks may come but it's best to reframe these circumstances until you see a solution and a path forward through prayer. With commitment, you find yourself as doing being.

2. ***Keep an open mind:***
   because open to the possibilities that exist for you. Open minded allows you experience life-changing people entering your life. They take an active role in helping you achieve your goals in life.

3. ***Be persistent:***
   The engine that keeps you going till you prevail is persistence. No matter the obstacles or dead ends you encounter along the way. Persistence is what keeps your legs strong when the waves keep crashing all around you. Persistence is your life ring, hope, the inner voice that coils and tells you never give up. Is also a choice.

4. ***Be flexible:***
   Also, know what is working for you and what seems not to. Learn to find a way to do more of what seem to work for you. It allows you to take the first step outside of your comfort zone. Waiting on other side is growth.

5. ***Have faith:***
   One thing that always keeps you going in other not to become weary is faith. Have faith in all you do. Your faith in god, you believe in you makes the difference. Also be careful about people who come around and tell you, you can't do it. Those are people with dreams yet settle for less.

Don't be deceived to be limited. If they are warning down in life, tell them you aren't. You are perusing to achieve your goals and purpose destined by God with faith. I promise you shall make it

6. ***Be thankful:***

Being thankful generator positive energy in and around you all the time. How do you turn things around when you not getting the positive results expected? Answer: show more gratitude for what you do have all the time then been disappointed by the things you do have. Consider all relationships in your life with people. You have the power to change any negative relationship to a more positive one by showing thankful.

7. ***Live your passion:***
   Live your dream. Love what you do. Do your best what you love. Your heart holds the deepest defiles and passions, these in pursuing them leads to happiness, success, and every fulfillment you deserve. find which your heart truly desire and follow it. Honor it and never give up on it. Keep listening to your heart and allow your passion to take you wherever it wants to. Your happiness will be waiting there!!!!.

Call For It

God still works miracles. Call for your miracle today right here and now. God needs his glory. He still works and performs a notable miracle through prayer. Because of deception, tricks, lies, in our church today makes it difficult for most Christians to believe and to think God still performs miracles. Well yes, he does. Only need to tell the spirits around and you shall know out of truth which of the miracles is of God. The Holy Spirit in existence puts us on the watch. Many miracles took place during the times of both mosses, Elijah and Elisha in the Old Testament. The gospel also records at least 35 miracles by Jesus Christ while the New Testament records many others that took place at hands of his disciples. Miracles were performing them. For example in acts chapter2" peter preached" men of Israel, hear these words; Jesus of Nazareth, a man attested to you by God did through him in your midst, as you yourselves know the same was true of apostles, as 2corinthians 12 note" the signs of a true apostle were performed among you with the utmost patience, with signs and wonders and mighty works. "Hebrew 2: 4" confirm while God also bore witness by signs and wonders and various miracles and by the gift of the Holy Spirit distributed according to his will". God is not done with miracles today. He still performs them. Miracles are something that occurs beyond natural explanation. God does still perform miracles. However, He does not need to duplicate the actions He has already performed that available for us to read in the Bible. Instead, we are called to study His word (2 Timothy 3:16-17) and apply its wisdom and teachings in our daily lives today.

Perhaps the best advice regarding the miracles of the Bible was given near the end of Johns Gospel. After years of following Jesus he wrote "Now Jesus did many others signs in the presence of the disciples which are not written in this book, but these are written so that you may believe that Jesus is the Christ, the son of God and that by believing you may have life in His name (John 20:30-31). The goal of miracle is ultimately for us in believing Jesus and to live for Him each day. Call for your miracle now. Is it barrenness? A skin disease that doctors have no idea of? Is it marriage? Are you suffering from serious menstrual pain, fibroids, all kind of tumors? Stroke, Deaf, Dump, Migraine, Poverty? Are you handicapped,?Are you possessed?Diabetic and so on? Call unto Jesus for you miracle right now!!! Keep praying

The Pattern Son

Jesus Christ of Nazareth is our pattern. He is the only way, light, truth. No onc goes to the father except through Him.
Jesus is Lord and savior. Bible teaches that we are to invite Him. "Phil 2:5" Is that what we are seeing in the churches across the world? Are we doing as He thought us? The life and worship today is now based on fame, wealth, power. People just chasing these not recognizing the dangers involved.Pastors, rushing to plant churches and making of names in deadly demonic ways deceiving mankind.Killings of the innocent soul for blood. I ask are these initiations monuments of Christ The pattern son? Are you embarrassed by God's way of salvation? (Rom 1:16,2Cor 6:). Will you not speak? And follow truth which is in Christ Jesus?People today in the church we look up to our compromising the truth and their own conviction. The walls of homes are broken. Walls of society is already broken and in chaos. Children are defenseless and vulnerable. The walls of the church are breaking. What is the difference between the Christian today, the unbeliever? The walls of morality have fallen down. The sanctity of marriages ruined. The gate of fidelity in marriages is burnt down. Even my own church is also having challenges too. Our heart today are filled with impurities, dishonoring our bodies, exchange the truth for a lie, pastors preaching their thoughts not of what God says, men given nature relation with human, kind of nature which is contrary to nature. It is time. Rise up to rebuild. Rise up help raise the burnt gates and walls for our children now!! May God help us to do this.

Now Imitate Jesus Christ

1 Corinthains11:1, 1peter 2:21 For this you were called because Christ also suffered for us. , Learning an example that you should follow His steps Ephes 5:15 Be an imitator of God, therefore as dearly loved children. John13:15 For I have given you an example, that you should do as I have done to you. John 2:6
He who says he abides in Him ought himself also to walk just as He walked 1John 2:6 The one who says he belongs to Christ should live the same kind of life Christ lived.

Love As Jesus Loved

John 13:34: “A new commandment I give to that you love one another as I have loved you, that you also love one another.

John 15:12 This is my commandment that you love one another as I have loved you

Becoming like Him. God's plan is to make you like Jesus 2Corinthians 3:18 Do the same works

John14:12. Most assuredly I say to you he who believes in me, the works that I do he will do also, and greater works than these he will do, I go to my father. You might think Jesus is an impossible pattern for us, humans, to follow. Well, we can never measure up to Jesus by ourselves. The only way is for us to yield to Jesus. To trust him completely and obey him explicitly.(The only way to be happy). In a sense, Jesus is living his life through us. We cannot do it by our own effort.

Gal 2:20 “ I have been crucified with Christ. It is no longer I who lives but Christ lives in me and the life which I now live in the flesh, I live by faith in the son of God which loved me and gave himself for me. Let Jesus live his life through you seek his guidance in everything then obey him.

Intimacy with The Holy Spirit

“ 1 THESSALONIANS 1:6” you become imitators of us and of the lord, for you welcomed the message in the midst of severe suffering with the joy is given by the holy spirit.

There are many Christians who realizing the poverty of their own spiritual life, given them to prayer for what is commonly called “revival”. What are they actually looking for? Some of our Christians brothers are asking for miraculous signs” developing a special vocabulary for example “baptism” of or in the holy spirit. I realize our churches of today are listening to Jesus Christ through the Holy Spirit but listening much to man's doctrines and sounds. Some really listen to their own emotions and the noises around them. Others are paying much attention to things happening in other communities and following them without hearing the principles of Christ released through the Holy Spirit. Our churches today are drawing in a tidal wave of imitating others instead of giving them the chance to listen to the Lord and his truth.

1. **The person of the holy spirit**

   The coming of the holy spirit is the fulfillment of the promise of Jesus Christ based on the words of Joel“ and afterward, I will pour out my spirit on all flesh” your sons and daughters will prophesy, your old men will dreams, your young men will see visions(Joel 2:28). In “ John 14:16,17” Jesus said to his disciples I will ask the father and he will give you another counselor to be with you forever. The spirit of truth. The word cannot accept him because it either sees him knows him but you know him for he lives with you and will be in you.

2. **Who is the holy spirit?**

   Most people see the holy spirit as a hidden power which can be released in favor of the one who uses the right formula. “the spirit is sometimes perceived as a force or an incomparable superior influence which causes the densest forest to tremble. Now the Holy Spirit is awesome. He is the third person of the Godhead. We find it associated with God the father, God the son, God the Holy Spirit.

Seven Ways to Develop Intimacy with the Holy Spirit

We all have heard individuals, groups who have been to the cave, rooms or wilderness spent a week with God and emerged on fire, powered up and talking about intimacy with the Holy Spirit. Special times spent in Gods presence are vital to those of us who want to grow in prophetic ministry. However, the reality is that for most of us, life is busy. We have families, jobs, and ministries that require daily time and attention.

With that in mind, there are some practical ways that we can develop intimacy with the Holy Spirit. Whilst going about our daily lives, family, businesses, and ministry. Here are 7 things that I have found helpful and I believe it will help you too.

1. Study what the Bible says about intimacy with the Holy Spirit. God's anointing, gifts, power are not sourced in an impersonal force or ability. They are the manifestation of a person.

The Holy Spirit.

Being grounded in scripture ensures that we have a strong foundation for developing an intimate relationship with the Holy Spirit. The Holy Spirit has a will and emotions. He has a voice and communicates in many ways.

2. Discover how you uniquely connect with the Holy Spirit and put all into practices Every relationship requires communication. Intimacy grows when we have special times together.Our relationship with God helps benefit from how we personally relate best to him. I value walking prayer outdoors. In the wide open space of creation, I have freedom to talk to my father and listen to the Holy Spirit without interruptions, however, it will be different for you. do you enjoy quiet times asides with God? Do you encounter him? How do you connect with him? Is it in the context of worship.Prayer, music?

3. Pay attention to; cultivate an awareness of the Holy Spirit. Bible says the Holy Spirit is present in and with us and so we believe it. He is our constant companion in most times in the bible God spoke to people in many different times not only when they were waiting on him, but also when they were traveling and working.

4. The Holy Spirit communicates with you right on the go. The moment you accept him. Relate to him in a natural way. There should be nothing strange or weird about our intimate relationship with the Holy spirit. It should provoke others to desire what we have, not put them off. Our relations with Him should be natural, life-giving, just as our relationship with the father and Jesus.

5. **Be real with God:**
   there's nothing to hide and no need to perform. A helpful word – play on intimacy is into me- see" You can be yourself, with both your strength and your weakness. He is our comforter and helper. We need to be closer to God, through prayer in His word to receive the assistance we desire.

6. **Practice Accountability in your spiritual Experiences**
   You can have a life with God that is lived in the context of community, and accountability. I regularly share descriptions of my encounters with God with my leaders and fellow prayer warriors. They help clarify what He is doing in my life and provide a means of accountability and growth. This is not always comfortable. However, I recognize that it is one of the most beneficial things I can do, is also biblical. As a result, there is no ceiling on my ministry and intimate relationship with God.

7. **Pray and ask for greater intimacy with the Holy Spirit:** Today, take the time to pray and ask God to stir up your desire for a greater level of encounter and intimacy with Him (Luke 11:9-13). Finally praying in the spirit is one of the most intimate encounters you can have with the Holy spirit. In those moments of prayer, invite the holy spirit to establish the father's purposes in your life and those who are in his heart (Jude 1:20, 1co 14:2, Rom 8:26)

CHAPTER FIVE

Your Birth Place of Testimonies

God is ever faithful. Being born again is my birth place of testimonies. Born again is described by many as the phenomenon of gaining faith in Jesus Christ. Is an experience when everything works for you and I. In John 3:3, Jesus answered and said to him verily, verily I say unto thee, Except a man be born again he can not see the kingdom of God. Jesus made this statement to Nicodemus who was a ruler of Jews. He heard Jesus preaching and he came to ask the same question probably you and I could have asked him then. How can a man be born again? Can he enter into his mother's womb? Jesus then answered that the new birth he was talking about wasn't physical but spiritual. The beginning of new life In a kingdom.The way back to God as our birthplace of testimonies or miracles is to acknowledge our need of a savior and accept Jesus Christ. God's love for us is not based upon our ability to come to him on our own merits. It is based on our acceptance that Jesus Christ paid the price for our sins. And there is nothing more for us to do. What do we turn to?

We turn to God who loves and cares for us. We turn to faith in Jesus Christ as our savior. Personally, his death on the cross, his burial, and his resurrection is my birthplace. That where I see all these salvation, notification, regeneration sanctification, righteousness, I Intendance, Romans 8.

Salvation
What good is it for a man to gain the whole world and yet loses or forfeit his soul or very self. "Luke 9:25" through our faith in Jesus Christ our lives are delivered from the terrible prospect of an eternity apart from God.finally this world salvation with all it entails, a perfect body a place in the new Jerusalem, rewards that last forever, perfect fellowship with all our brothers and sisters, and the greatest blessing of all. Truly this is a price worth winning.

Justification
The right of our faith as being righteous in the sight of God. Is also od's act of removing every guilt of sin through Christ Jesus, atoning sacrifice

Regeneration
Rebirth or born again is when we are made brand new, formed, spiritually, holy, a heavenly birth that results in our being made alive.

Sanctification
The sanctity of us is being made holy to be functioning so well as Christians. The blood upon his death purifies and frees us from sin. Our actual lives become increasing confirmed with our legal status before God.

Righteousness
Is different from holiness. Righteousness is one of the key attributes of God as portrayed in the Hebrew bible. God spotters holiness, His perfect obedience John 17:25, Deut. 25: 1, Psalm 1:6

Inheritance
The believer's inheritance is for the children, who are partakers of the knowledge of redemption, but of God, and joint- heirs with Christ Jesus "Rom. 8:17". Note property in this world usually goes by inheritance, but it is not so with Heavens highest blessings. They are of blood, neither of the will of man, but of God.

Born verses Born Again

Born is when a person is by birth naturally. People are born with various types of tribes, religions, homes, families. This is different from born again. To be born again is to accept a life of hope and truth in Christ Jesus. Many people think they know all it means to be born again. Others born into the Christian religion think it ends there so far as you are born a Christian. A born again Christian is someone who has repented of their sins and turn to Christ for their salvation. As a result has become part of Gods family forever. All this takes place as God spirit works in our lives. To be born by nature denies you as a member of God's family which prevents you from inheriting God's internal life. My prayer is that you too may be born again and become part of God's family. By a simple prayer of faith, tell God that you know you are a sinner, and you are sorry for your sins. Then ask Christ Jesus to come into your life and save you. When you do, God will come to live within you by His spirit, and you will be born again.

Amen

Existing vs. Living

We exist because we are alive and living. Relatively speaking, there a difference between living (as in leading a life we enjoy or what) and serving (as in living through one set of trouble to another).

Differences between living and existing.

I feel and think the biggest distinction between living and existing is how much control a person have over life decisions. Where do you see control coming from? In general, someone who existing feels as everything is outside of their control, living knows they determine the path their life takes. Emotions such as fear and anger dictate what they can and can't do. Someone who is living controls them and doesn't let them interfere with their decisions. Someone who exists would stay in the same dead end job for years despite being unsatisfied and unhappy. Their fears trapped them and they have no plans of getting out.

People who simply exist do the same boring routine every day even though they don't really like it. They don't take, any chances of improving their life just so they can maintain their current comfortable lifestyle. This is because they are unable to take control of their decision. How to stop existing and start living.

How would you know if you are existing on living?

- If you not getting excited or happy most days with what you're going to do, you need to take action and change something. This should affect every area of your life.

- If you have yourself saying no to a question most offer then you need to make a change to confront those fears holding you back and remind yourself that change is necessary.

- The benefit of Divine direction is an honor, beauty, dignity, and story. These make you envied by other men. It also gets things done so cheaply for you. Whilst another struggle, you don't.

- No force if hell can ever stop a man who discovers the angel's charge over you, to cut off any advising that dares to come near. Should even fall on swords, they will not be able to wound you, because the Lords stand strongly behind you thank Him. You shall outshine all earthly stars, because of the mighty hand of God behind, operating on your behalf. Just thank Him.

- Nobody who locates the ways of Gods leading will thank Him for taking you to high places in life

- Divine direction eases life for you. It makes life cheaper for you. It makes you enjoy divine backing. It makes you extraordinary among people.

- They say Happiness is not found, it is created. If you're not a happy person of God, you will never be a winning person. In this life, it is compulsory to be happy, very dangerous to be gloomy or sad. If you want to win in life then be joyful.

- Until there's a song in your heart, you'll never hear the sound from heaven. Nothing is more colorful than divine guidance. They are out to destroy whatever causing sorrow around you, It takes a good ear to hear a sound from heaven. A sound from above comes with a blessing for you. I welcome you to a word of dignity. Dignity comes by embracing heavenly instructions and adhering to them, not minding human comments or condemnation.

- All you have to do is to stay heed to your assignment and you will never know the lack of anything. All you need is to be obedient, that will bring you plenty of divine manifestations.

- The path of a man who is doing it right shines brighter and brighter. But the path of the just is as the shining light that shined more unto the perfect day.

Some years back I went through something similar in a job. I was offered. It was horrible but after several months of work, I realized I had started going there only because of habit and not because I like the work itself. Someone forced me into accepting that kind of job. I know I needed so quit. I had searched for a job before I left, but didn't have anything lined up right away. It was so scary at first, but I knew quitting was the right thing to do. So a year later I was still glad I made the decision. Be in control of your life. In the end, you will be the one to make decisions for your life. Nothing should tell you what to do, not even your fears and doubts.

Do you think you are living or existing? Are there things you've become comfortable with and need to make changes?

Purpose for Living

Somebody may ask "what is the purpose for living if you know at the end of it all, you are going to die and not remember anything?

You should know in this life no one lives forever. Seriously why do most people think money is the only way to worship and serve him? He is to be a part of our lives; in busy times, quiet spaces and during night hours.

No moment of our lives should be off limit with seeking the Lord first.

"Seek ye first the kingdom of God"
"And his righteousness"
"And everything shall be added unto you".

TESTIMONY

There was this woman on anxiety and high blood pressure indication.She suffered so very much for over 10years, taken the pills prescribed by the doctor then one day she had the conviction to end all that by holding up high unto God for His final say on her situation. As she made up her mind to learn, pray God's word with faith, she was introduced by a close friend of mine. As we prayed to God with faith, she got healed by the power in the blood and name Jesus. That sickness puts her in a serious chase to seek God. She realized except God saves her, no man can only Jesus can save you as I write this she's living as a normal woman sickness free, which now to the glory of God eats normally. She eats everything. You too need Jesus in your situation now.

Remember no voodoo, witchcraft, sorcery and so on can save you.

I encourage every person, reader or not, Christian, student, pastor or minister of God to read this book and receive God's insight into your spirit being as a seed planted inside you to produce a well devoted spiritual harvest. It will also help you know what's happening in this dispensation of our world and to know and to have knowledge on everything to pray effectively to God for answers. I also edge you to desire the gift of praying in the Holy Spirit if you are not baptized yet. The Holy Spirit teaches all things Let this be a guide for you today.

THE OTHER SIDE OF PRAYER……
Amen.

Inspirational quotes

1. Still there, Praise there, I decree that you are coming out in the name of Jesus.
2. There's no failure in God, Expect a miracle now!!!
3. He is still working on me but so far, I love what The Lord has done. Do it again Lord.
4. God is ready with your miracle. Are you ready?
5. The Spirit of the Lord says you are due for another breakthrough.
6. The heart of the king is in God's hands and He turns it where He wills.
7. Trust God in His presence everything gets fixed. Just get there.
8. Where you are is a blessing.
9. Someone is in a worse place. Thank God for your situation.
10. This is a great day to live life more abundantly. Think about it.
11. You are loaded with benefits.
12. There are more for you than against you.
13. You have favor with God and man.
14. Favor is calling your name. So step up now!!
15. In Him is where you belong.
16. You have recognized in a higher place in the heavens. Arise!!
17. Your income shall increase because your lifestyle change has been ordered.
18. Some places in life are temporary. Don't tabernacle there.
19. Time for greater assets from the kingdom
20. Your vision shall cause you to pray for a greater capacity.
21. Is your season to receive
22. I prophesy your season of returns
23. The reaping anointing is released.
24. You attract what you honors
25. The oil is about to just flow for somebody
26. Leaders it is in you to bless the people. People please pull on the anointing

27. So God is restoring the years for you beginning right now. It won't take long.
28. Covenant secured you're your spot even when you got weak. God remembers
29. Return to Him now!!!
30. Just be ready to receive. This is your due season. Shine forever.
31. As you read whatever you do shall prosper.
32. Real church members tithe and attend almost every scheduled service.

26169467R00042

Printed in Great Britain
by Amazon